D1523343

I WANT TO KNOW ABOUT
A FLIGHT TO THE MOON

I WANT TO KNOW ABOUT

A FLIGHT TO THE
MOON

Col. Alfred M. Worden

with an Introduction by Fred Rogers
of Mister Rogers' Neighborhood

Produced and developed by
Whitehall, Hadlyme & Smith, Inc.

DOUBLEDAY & COMPANY, INC.
GARDEN CITY, NEW YORK

Photo Credits
Sherman C. Holaday, Jr., p. 6
National Aeronautics and Space Administration, p. 2, 15, 16, 18, 19, 22, 23, 24, 26, 27, 28, 30, 31, 33, 35, 36, 37, 38, 41, 43, 44, 45, 47, 49, 50, 52, 54, 55, 58.

Library of Congress Cataloging in Publication Data

Worden, Alfred Merrill.
    I want to know about a flight to the moon.

    SUMMARY: A member of the Apollo 15 crew describes how he became an astronaut, the training he received, and the flight of the Apollo 15.
    1. Project Apollo—Juvenile literature. 2. Space flight to the moon—Juvenile literature. 3. Worden, Alfred Merrill—Juvenile literature. [1. Project Apollo. 2. Space flight to the moon. 3. Worden, Alfred Merrill] I. Title.
TL789.8.U6A67   629.45'4'0924[B]
ISBN: 0-385-04682-0
ISBN: 0-385-05837-3 (lib. bdg.)
Library of Congress Catalog Card Number 73–21878

INTRODUCTION

Al Worden is the first poet to have ever flown to the moon! Of course he's a great scientist, but one of the great things about him is that he uses his gift of communication to make traveling in space so much more comprehensible to those of us who stay on the earth.

"Did anybody tell you that you *had* to go to the moon?"

"What do you eat up there?"

"How do you go to the bathroom in space?"

. . . all questions that young people ask with frankness and real interest. Al Worden answers them and many more in this very personal "conversation" with his reader.

When I look at the moon, I often think of things that Al has told my family and me about his Apollo mission. I'm glad that he has taken the time to write this book for all of us who care about human beings and our world and anything which may help us understand and plan ahead.

FRED ROGERS

PREFACE

It took a long time for this book to come into being. In fact, the whole thing began even before my flight on Apollo 15 in July 1971.

I felt very strongly that the launch of a manned spacecraft was something that all children should see. However, since it was impossible for them to come to Cape Kennedy to watch the actual lift-off, I decided to try to have them watch it through the eyes of a friend, Mr. Fred Rogers. So I called Mr. Rogers at his show, "Mister Rogers' Neighborhood," and explained my idea to him. He was delighted with the thought of filming the launch for his children. He came down to the Cape before lift-off and we spent a day talking about the flight and filming one for his TV programs. He brought with him a lot of questions that had been sent to him by the young people who watch his program, and part of the show was my answers to those questions.

After the flight I got the idea that it might be worthwhile to write a book about space travel. And it might be a better idea if the book could be based on questions that children have actually asked me. Since that time I have talked to countless groups of youngsters from New York to California, keeping a record of the things that they seemed most interested in.

So here is the book. It contains the information that hundreds of children have asked for.

I WANT TO KNOW ABOUT
A FLIGHT TO THE MOON

Here I am with my two sisters. Sally is on the left and Carolyn is on the right. I was four years old at the time.

I was born and raised in Jackson, Michigan, where my father and mother still live. I was the second oldest in a family of six children, and most of our growing-up years were spent on a small farm just outside of town. My two sisters, three brothers, and I all attended a small one-room country school just down the road from our farm. There were about thirty students in the school, which went from kindergarten to the eighth grade. When I got old enough, it became my job to go to the school early in the morning and build a fire in the stove so the school would be warm when classes started. Then I would go back home and do the regular chores, such as milking the cows and feeding all the animals. At one time we had four cows, three horses, pigs, chickens, ducks, cats, and dogs.

When there are six children in the family, there are bound to be a lot of arguments, and we certainly had our share. Yet, as I look back, I realize that we were almost always able to work out our problems on our own. Only once in a while did our parents have to step into an argument and settle it.

One advantage we had that few children have—our father worked in a movie theater. Many was the time that we watched movies with him when we were little.

As I grew older my interests changed and my desire to go to college increased. I wanted to go to college and learn all about music. I had taken piano lessons since I was five years old, and it seemed natural that I continue with music. However, because our family was so large, my parents could not afford to pay for my college education. So I applied to go to West Point, the United States Military Academy. When I was accepted at West Point, I gave up on a music career and began looking forward to life in the military.

Here is a family picture when I was about eighteen. Top row: Jim, Sally, me, Carolyn. Bottom row: Jerry, Dad, Mother, Peter.

The Academy not only taught me the academic courses required to be a good officer, but it also taught me a sense of self-discipline and the motivation to do the best I could in my job.

I went into the Air Force after graduation and learned how to fly, something I had always wanted to do. Somehow, flying combines all the best things a young man wants. There is a freedom in being able to soar in the sky, and yet it takes a great deal of knowledge and discipline to do it safely and easily. The more I flew, the more I wanted to know about airplanes, so I went back to college to learn all I could. Part of the course was about rockets, and that was the start of my interest in being an astronaut.

In this picture I was about twenty-one and attending the United States Military Academy at West Point.

Going to school is important for young people because it allows them to learn more about the things they are interested in and prepares them better to take advantage of opportunities. I don't think I would have been prepared well enough to be selected as an astronaut if I hadn't gone back to college for more study. But because I did go back, I was ready when NASA was selecting more crewmen to go to the moon.

Now I have children of my own—both of them girls. Merrill, the older one, wants to be a veterinarian—an animal doctor—one day. I think she will be a very good one, because of her love for animals. Her mother and I will certainly support and encourage her. Alison, my younger daughter, hasn't yet decided what she wants to do, but she has several years before she graduates from high school so there is lots of time. I don't think either of them wants to be an astronaut.

But I think that they were proud of me when I went on the Apollo 15 flight. On the other hand, they were also a little frightened. They were proud because there was a lot of publicity on TV and in the newspapers and magazines. And they were frightened because they know how far away the moon is and because they thought it was very dangerous for me to go there.

One thing that everybody seems to wonder about is why people go to the moon in the first place. One of the things I believe is that we go to the moon so we can find out more about ourselves. We also want to find out more about the moon and our own planet, the earth. And the more we know, the more we will be able to make the earth a better place in which to live.

Besides that, we are concerned for the future. We want to improve things for people who have not even been born yet. Ever since we started the moon program, we have been thinking of how to make life better for people who won't be born for another hundred years or more.

And then there is the old pioneering spirit. The desire to explore new territory. Why did Columbus go on his voyages? Because he wanted to discover a new way to the East. Because he wanted to prove that the earth was round like a ball. Because he wanted to go some place that no one had ever been before.

With my two daughters—Merrill is on the left and Alison is on the right.

The Apollo 15 crew—left to right: Scott, Worden, Irwin.

To become an astronaut you have to have a few more quali-
fications than Columbus' sailors had. You must have a college
degree and you must have a certain amount of flying time in
various kinds of airplanes, especially jets.

Then you have to be a certain age. Of course, someone who
is eighteen years old does not have a college degree and a lot
of flying time logged. Someone who is sixty years old is usually
not in as good physical shape as someone who is younger. So
there is an age cutoff for application to the program, and it is
thirty-five.

By the way, women, unfortunately, do not often have the required amount of jet flying time, so this is probably the reason that we have had no women astronauts. I am certain that this will change, however.

Nobody said that I had to fly to the moon. It was my choice to apply for the program. But once I was accepted and assigned to a crew, it was no longer my choice. That was the crew I was on and that was the crew with whom I would go to the moon.

I sometimes wonder if I would have liked to walk on the moon. I guess it would have been fun, but I wasn't trained to do it. We didn't switch jobs on the crew. Everyone was prepared to do a particular job. And that decision was made about three years before we blasted off.

I'm not sure that there was any conscious effort made to select a particular characteristic or quality that would make anyone the best choice for a certain job. The selection was done at random. But when it was done, it was done. This man goes into orbit—this man goes on the moon's surface.

It happened this way. You may have heard that in 1967 we had a big fire at the Cape. And we lost three of our fellow astronauts who were sitting in a spacecraft on the launch pad. We had a very large rebuilding program after that, and we went back and redesigned a lot of things in the spacecraft.

The thing that we worked hardest on redesigning was the command module—the part of the spacecraft that we went out in and back in. The three dead men had been in the command module at the time of the fire, and that's where the trouble was.

Well, my job was to work with the people who were redesigning the command module. I spent two years working with the company that built it, helping to rebuild it so that it would be safe. That gave me a lot of background. In fact, I ended up knowing all of the systems that make it work. So it was natural for me to fly it. Especially since there would be that long time when one man would be alone, circling the moon, while the other two were on the moon itself.

This is an excellent view of the Apollo 15 command and service module in lunar orbit. The photograph was taken by Jim Irwin from the lunar module during rendezvous.

It's crowded in there.

Dave Scott and Jim Irwin, then, trained for walking on the moon, driving the Rover, and flying the lunar module.

When you sum it up, it might be that it is a set of circumstances rather than qualities that make one man a moonwalker and another a moon-orbiter.

There is one thing that ought to be pointed out. Astronauts are human. We all have our various habits—bad and good. Probably all of us feel like crying sometimes, or losing our tempers, or playing hooky from our jobs.

As a matter of fact, we were not always happy with each other. We are friends, of course, but we were never really close friends. By that I mean that I didn't go over to Dave or Jim's house every night to have dinner. And we didn't go to movies together or anything like that.

But on the job we worked well together. One important thing to know is that you don't have to be close friends to work well together. I'm not even sure that I would have wanted my best friend to fly to the moon with me.

Out in space you don't get on each other's nerves. Even when one of your companions leaves the cap off the toothpaste. You feel that what you are doing is so much more important than being irritated by little things. Sure, when we were on the ground we argued about many things. Sometimes it seemed that we never agreed about anything. That's natural.

But in flight we all had a job to do and we were all trying to do it well by working together. So there were no arguments and very few discussions. We got along very well because we all had our own job to do. When you are two hundred thousand miles from the earth, it is kind of silly to argue with somebody. It doesn't help. But when we got back to earth . . .

In training, we have to learn about a lot of things. Not only how to run the equipment, but also what to do in case something goes wrong. Suppose that we go out on a flight and we are in lunar orbit. Suppose that the engine fails to fire when we are ready to return to earth? We will be stuck in solar orbit forever, so what do we do? Do we take a little poison pill so that we will die quickly instead of waiting around until our oxygen is used up?

No, we don't. The thing that would happen is that as the oxygen ran out, we would go into a permanent sleep. But we didn't go out there thinking that we were going to get stuck in space. We went out there confident that the system was built so well that nothing would go wrong.

Of course, we knew that if we got in that kind of trouble, it would be impossible for another rocket to fly up to save us. There just wouldn't be a rocket ready to go.

Human failure was always a possibility, and we were trained to cope with it. For example, one man could bring the command module back even if the other two were sick or dead. And we trained one man to fly both spacecraft. I was trained to fly the command module. Jim Irwin was trained to fly the lunar module. And Dave Scott was trained to fly both.

If I became sick, Dave could fly the command module. If Jim became sick, Dave could fly the lunar module. Unfortunately, if Dave and Jim both became sick on the moon while I was orbiting, there would be nothing I could do to help them. I often thought that if that happened, I would keep on orbiting until I was sure that they could not be saved, and then head for home. I was trained to fly the command module alone, but it would have been a lonely trip.

The biggest problem, obviously, would be Jim's if Dave and I both became sick. He could get Dave back to the command module, but he didn't know how to fly it. Fortunately, the men on the earth could have talked him down, but it would have taken a lot out of him.

The reason that all three of us were not taught how to fly both modules was one of time. We trained three years as it was just to learn the job that we were assigned to. It would have taken another year and a half to train everybody well enough to fly both.

Another thing that we worried about was what would happen if the engines quit during launch. We spent a lot of time training for just that. The part of the spacecraft that we lived in during the flight could be ejected from the rest of the craft. You have seen pictures of that big tower that is attached to

There's always a lot to think about.

Lightning struck near the Apollo 15 Saturn V space vehicle during pre-launch preparations.

Part of the emergency survival training.

the top of the command module. That's an escape tower that can pull the whole spacecraft up. It can go quite high in the air by itself. Then we would get rid of the tower and parachute to the ground.

But suppose that the spacecraft just started to tip over before we blasted off? There is an automatic system that watches all of these kinds of things. If the booster should start to tip over, the system would fire the launch escape tower rockets and we would be off in the air. And if, during the launch the booster began to curve back toward the earth, our capsule would also be ejected and we would parachute down.

We also put in a lot of time in emergency survival training. We do that in case we should come down on land someplace instead of in the water. We learned how to build shelters with our parachutes. We went through jungle training. The main thing was to learn to survive until we could be rescued.

Then there was the time spent on learning to drive the Rover. That's the little car that was made to ride around on over the surface of the moon. It didn't take up much space in the spacecraft, because it folded up like a suitcase. Of course it's pretty big for a suitcase—about five feet long and four feet wide. And it weighs about four hundred pounds. When it comes time to unfold it, all you have to do is to pull a cord on the side of the lunar module and it comes right out. Then the tires fold out, and the Rover sits there, ready to go.

The tires, incidentally, are about the same size as car tires, but they are not made of rubber. Instead, they are woven out of piano wire. That's why they kick up dust on the lunar surface, and why we had to build fenders over each tire to keep the dust away from Dave and Jim. Even then, their suits were pretty dirty when they finally left the moon.

The Rover is pretty slow. Usually it is driven at about seven miles an hour, and it probably will not do better than ten. That's why you couldn't drive it over to the other side of the moon. It would take so long to get there that the Rover would run out of battery power.

I mentioned that the Rover weighs about four hundred pounds. But those are earth pounds. On the moon, things

On the left, Jim Irwin sets up the Apollo lunar surface experiments package during practice run. And on the right he is setting up the suprathermal ion detector experiment.

Here is the lunar roving vehicle on the moon.

weigh only about one sixth of what they would weigh on the earth. That is caused by the lesser force of gravity on the moon. So the Rover weighs only about sixty-five pounds when it is on the moon. And that is about the most expensive sixty-five pounds that you can imagine. The Rover that we carried on our flight cost between five hundred thousand and six hundred thousand dollars.

I should say a word about the computers we used during our flight. Both the command module and the lunar module had computers. These computers could solve the equations that told us how to change our course to go into lunar orbit, land on the moon, then rendezvous and return to earth. The computer could also help us make those course changes by turning the engines on and off at the right times, but only if we told it to do that for us. In fact, computers can't do anything until someone tells them what to do. We even used computers during the launch from Cape Kennedy to monitor our flight and tell the ground controllers if something was wrong. Fortunately, nothing went wrong during our launch. We did have a couple of small problems during the flight, such as a water leak, but these problems didn't involve our computers.

Many people ask me about the space suits that we wore on the mission. On the ground we had a great deal of trouble walking about in them. They weigh about eighty pounds. But on the moon, they weigh between thirteen and fourteen pounds and are much easier to get around in.

When it was time to get into our space suits, we helped each other. We had two different kinds of suits on Apollo 15, one for the two men that went to surface and another for the one that stayed in orbit. Dave and Jim needed suits that would bend at the waist so they could drive the Rover and bend down to pick up rocks. My suit did not have that kind of mobility, but it was built so I could get into it by myself. Dave and Jim had to help each other into their suits.

The first thing we put on was a set of long underwear, to help keep us warm and to keep the suit from rubbing directly against our skin. The underwear also protected the medical

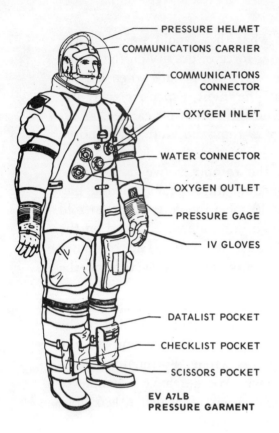

PRESSURE HELMET
COMMUNICATIONS CARRIER
COMMUNICATIONS CONNECTOR
OXYGEN INLET
WATER CONNECTOR
OXYGEN OUTLET
PRESSURE GAGE
IV GLOVES
DATALIST POCKET
CHECKLIST POCKET
SCISSORS POCKET

EV A7LB
PRESSURE GARMENT

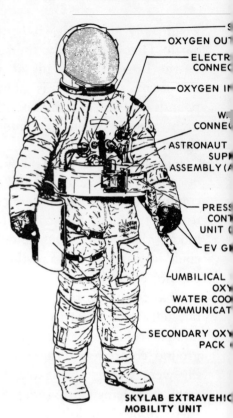

S
OXYGEN OUT
ELECTR
CONNEC
OXYGEN IN
W.
CONNEC
ASTRONAUT
SUPF
ASSEMBLY (A
PRESS
CONT
UNIT (
EV G
UMBILICAL
OXY
WATER COO
COMMUNICAT
SECONDARY OXY
PACK

SKYLAB EXTRAVEHIC
MOBILITY UNIT

sensors we wore that let the doctors in Houston keep an eye on our physical condition. Then we put our feet in the legs of the space suit and pulled it up as far as we could while sitting down. Next, we stood up and put on the rest of the suit as if we were putting on a heavy overcoat. Then we stood up straight to pull the suit tight, closed all the zippers, and connected the oxygen and communication umbilicals. Finally, we put the radio earphones and microphones on our heads and put on the gloves and helmet. We were very careful with the space suit while we put it on, and it usually took twenty minutes or so.

Space suits are white because the color white reflects the rays of the sun. In space there is no atmosphere, which means we get the full impact of the sun's rays. If the suits were some other color, they would absorb more of the sun's rays and they

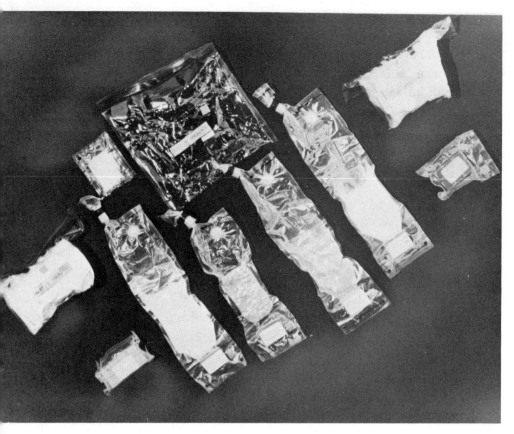

The Apollo food as packaged for flight.

would be quite hot inside. So in addition to providing us with an atmosphere, the suits also protect us from the sun.

We wore the space suits when we were being launched, when we were going through an open hatch, and at certain other times. That is, only when there was any question about keeping the atmosphere around us in a healthy condition. The rest of the time we took off the suits and traveled in our coveralls.

You might expect us to get very thirsty during a space flight and you might wonder where we get our water. First of all, we carry our own water with us. And we are able to manufacture it as we go. We have a thing called a "fuel cell" which takes hydrogen and oxygen from tanks and combines them in a complicated way.

The result is that there is a reaction that creates electrical power and also produces water. The water is pumped into a tank and we use it to drink. So we get water and electricity at the same time.

And it's just like home. We have hot water and cold water at the same time.

When we got bored with plain water to drink, we could switch to something else. We had powdered drinks in plastic bags—just like the powdered orange juice that you may have at breakfast. We would put water inside the plastic bag and mix it all up. Then we would put a little hole in the bag and drink it. We couldn't put it into a cup because if we did, the water would all float out.

As for the food, it tasted just like any other food. It was probably a little more expensive than the food that you eat at your table because it was prepared especially for the flight. It was dried and placed in plastic bags that were put on board the spacecraft. When we were ready to eat, we added water to the bag, let it mix with the food, and it became just as nourishing as the food we eat on earth.

Sometimes we ate hamburgers and hot dogs. These were precooked and packaged in aluminum bags that were something like sandwich bags. All we had to do was to cut the end off a bag and take the hamburger or hot dog out and eat it. It was almost like carrying your lunch to school.

Then there were the space food sticks. These were manufactured for the first time for the Apollo 15 flight.

Before we blasted off, I thought that I would have to learn how to eat all over again. After all, there is no gravity inside the capsule. And I thought that food would be hard to swallow. But the body is an interesting thing. It seems to adapt very quickly, and I never had any difficulty swallowing in space.

In a way, the food we ate was like the food you take with you when you are backpacking. And the lobster salad and shrimp salad was really delicious.

Before we left the earth, a diet was set up for us that gave us the proper amount of calories for the time that we were to be away. It worked out very well. I lost only three pounds, which isn't bad for a twelve-day trip.

Of course, body processes do not stop when you are in space, so some arrangements had to be made so that we could go to the bathroom. As far as liquid wastes are concerned, we got rid of them by piping them outside the spacecraft. But the solid wastes had to be put in plastic bags and saved until we returned to earth.

We couldn't put the solid wastes in a refrigerator because there wasn't one on board. But something will have to be done if we ever go to Mars or some other planet. The solid wastes could not be saved on a trip that might last for a year and a half. Perhaps some kind of a compartment might be built so that it could be exposed to a vacuum and dried out.

Here's our prelaunch breakfast. From left to right: Charles Buckley, Kennedy Space Center security chief; me; David R. Scott, mission commander; Donald K. Slayton, chief of Flight Crew Operations at the Manned Spacecraft Center; and Harrison H. Schmitt, Apollo 15 backup lunar module pilot.

When the time came, we were ready to make the flight. After we put on our space suits the morning of launch, we had to undergo treatment to prevent the bends. This is the same condition that divers sometimes get when they come up through the water too fast. The nitrogen in their body starts to make bigger and bigger bubbles, and it is very painful and can be fatal.

Of course, this could also happen to an astronaut in the reduced pressure of the capsule. So the plan was to get most of the nitrogen out of the body before blast off. Nitrogen is a gas that does not combine with anything in the bloodstream. But it can form little bubbles in the blood. And it is always there, as long as you breathe air in our atmosphere. You see, atmosphere is about four fifths nitrogen.

As you fly higher and higher, the pressure on the outside of your body gets less than the pressure on the inside of your body. So the nitrogen makes bigger and bigger bubbles. The secret of getting rid of most of the nitrogen is to breathe pure oxygen for a while. Over the years, doctors have made some pretty accurate charts that show exactly how much nitrogen you lose for every minute you are breathing pure oxygen. It takes about three hours of this to get the required amount of nitrogen out of your system.

Oxygen, which we breathed during the flight, behaves differently from nitrogen. The body uses it to liberate energy inside the body. It combines with the food that you eat to do this.

The date was July 26, 1971, and we were ready to suit up. Early in the morning we went into a large, very clean, room to put on our space suits. We had to stay in the suits for several hours before launch to make sure that we had been breathing pure oxygen long enough to remove the nitrogen in our blood. While this was going on, Jim Irwin put a towel over his head and went to sleep.

When we finished pre-breathing oxygen, they put us in a van and took us out to the launch pad. Then we got inside the command module and waited. And waited. And waited.

34

Here I am having my space suit pressure checked.

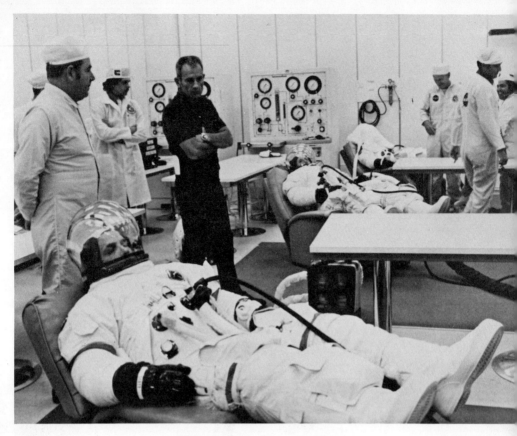

Then we relax for several hours.

In the weeks before the launch I thought that I would probably be very frightened. We were going a long way from the earth. We would be in a very small compartment. Certainly we would be lonely. And we would be in touch with other people only by radio.

But when we got inside the capsule, a strange thing happened. We had to sit in there for about two and a half hours before launch. For the first twenty minutes or so we were pretty excited. But it was dark and cold inside and we were a little sleepy. This was probably a nervous reaction to what was going on. I know that I was yawning.

So there we were. Sitting on top of a tall rocket. That's a lot like sitting in a room on the fortieth floor of a building. It's a long way to the ground. About every half hour there would be something to do that would keep you awake. But the excite-

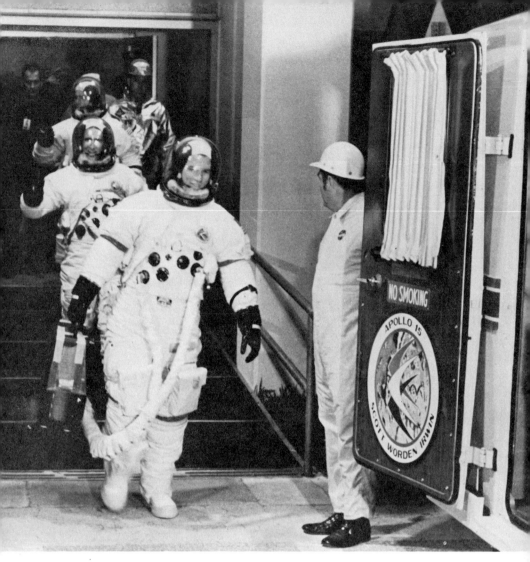

Now it's off to the launch pad.

ment didn't really begin until about twenty minutes before launch. Then things got very busy and we really didn't have a chance to think about much until the last thirty seconds of the countdown.

You can see the fire from the rocket engine at about T—7 seconds. Then comes the lift-off at T—o and you are on the way.

Of course, you know from telecasts of Apollo launches that the rocket makes a lot of noise at take-off. But the funny thing

37

The lift-off of Apollo 15.

is that it does not seem so loud inside the command module. Remember that we were moving away from the noise and the noise was coming from a place about three hundred feet behind us. That's the length of a football field. As a matter of fact, the ship didn't vibrate as much as I had expected it too, either.

After a short time, the first stage of the rocket was ready to be jettisoned, or dropped. The engineers that built the booster have handled this very well. Just before the first stage ran out of fuel, and they knew exactly when that would happen, the engines were shut down and the stage was dropped. Then the engines in the next stage were ready to take over. The whole thing was accurate to the split second.

So many people ask about the effects of gravity in space that I had better talk about that right here. On the earth we are used to the force of gravity. And we call the normal earth force of gravity "1 G." That's what makes us weigh what we weigh. That's what keeps us down on the ground. If there weren't any gravity, you wouldn't be able to walk around.

You know how it is sometimes in a car when you pull away from a stop light very fast? You feel as though you are being pushed against the back of your seat. That's called "acceleration." And it is similar to the force of gravity.

Now when we were sitting on the launch pad, we weighed exactly what we weighed on earth. The force of gravity was about the same as on the ground.

But when we blasted off and went faster and faster through the sky, the acceleration made it feel as if the force of gravity had increased. For about two minutes and forty seconds—up to the end of the first stage—we really felt the force of gravity increasing. Up to something like $4\frac{1}{2}$ Gs. That means it felt as if we weighed four and one half times what we weighed on earth.

It felt as if three and one half people were sitting on top of us. It was kind of unpleasant. But it wasn't as bad as you may have thought when you were watching some science fiction movies on television.

When we were on our way through space, outside the earth's atmosphere, there was no gravity at all inside the spacecraft.

It felt a little the way you feel when you are swimming under water. Only we couldn't come up at all. And there was another difference, of course. We didn't have any water to float through.

When you are swimming, you can pull yourself in one direction, and if you want to turn around, you can turn around. You are really pushing your hands against the water and it turns you around. In space there isn't anything like water to push against. You can't guide yourself. You can't lie down. There isn't any down.

So for twelve days I just floated. Sometimes we had a little fun, such as turning somersaults. We would float in the spacecraft and starting turning very slowly and then pull our knees up under our chins. We would just spin and spin and never stop until we hit something solid.

Everything in the spacecraft that is not pinned down will float. So when you want to sit down in your seat, you have to use a seat belt.

Of course, when they landed on the moon, Jim and Dave felt the pull of the moon's gravity. Remember that that is about one sixth of the earth's gravity. But I was without this feeling for the whole trip.

As we were rising through the earth's atmosphere and looked toward the moon, the sky seemed to become darker and darker. We could still see the moon and stars, but the area around them became jet black. That was at the point when we left the earth's atmosphere. Once you get out there, there is nothing to diffuse the rays of the sun and stars, so everything else looks black.

I rather liked it out there. It's very quiet and there are not many people around.

On the way there was a lot to do. And it was done by the clock. Of course, we couldn't depend on earth time out there. What time zone would we have been in? But we did have a clock that started counting at zero when we lifted off and just kept counting all the time. The clock had no hands—just numbers that kept flashing.

We had to do a lot of observing. For instance, did you know that the earth doesn't seem to change color? That's because

Jim Irwin took this shot of Dave Scott working near the Rover at the Apollo 15 landing site.

it has an atmosphere around it. And you can't see it rotate because it does that so slowly. Of course, if you watched it for two or three hours, you would probably notice some rotation. But if you just looked out the window once in a while, it would look as if it were just sitting there and not moving.

We could tell the difference between the continents and the oceans, but it didn't always look like your map of the earth. Sometimes clouds would cover the land and the ocean. I remember seeing a little bit of the Sahara Desert, Florida, and

South America when there weren't any clouds over them. And what I could see looked just as I thought it would. I developed a lot of respect for the people who draw maps.

At this point of the flight we were still moving very fast. When we left earth orbit we were going at about twenty-five thousand miles per hour. Then we slowed down, to about three thousand miles per hour at the point where the moon's gravity just equaled the earth's gravity. As we got closer to the moon we began speeding up again because of the gravitational pull of the moon. The men on earth were keeping track of our position, but we had no sensation of movement. First of all, we were in a zero-G environment. We were floating inside. Secondly, we had nothing going by us to tell us how fast we were traveling or to act as a point of reference.

When you are in a car, driving down the highway, how do you know that you are moving? You see trees, buildings, and other things going by. But up there, there's no air and no trees or buildings and no ground going past. The stars, the moon, and the earth are so far away you don't really see them move. It's as if you were standing still.

Finally we got to a place where we could begin to see the actual surface of the moon. This was a little scary. But you might be a little scared if you lived in a big city all your life and suddenly were flown out over the desert. That would be quite an experience. Add to this the fact that you know you are a long way from home, and it does make it kind of scary. However, we had complete confidence in the men at Mission Control and in our spacecraft, so we weren't really frightened.

We took a lot of pictures of the moon's surface, and they all came out a different color. The moon is a different color depending on which way you look at it. If you look at the moon up close with the sun at your back, it is a different color than if you look at it with the sun in front of you. And it's a different color again if you look at the surface of the moon with the sun on either side of you. The brightness of the moon does change for us here on earth depending on whether you look at it during the day or the night.

I could make up a display of pictures that we took of the

I took this picture of the far side of the moon from the command module
while I was in orbit.

It does look like a desert, doesn't it?

moon's surface and show you all different shades. Some are very brown and some are very gray. And they were taken of the same area of the moon. The color never goes to pink, only between gray and brown. But it depends on what angle the sun's rays are striking it.

That is, for the part of the moon that we call the lighted side. Because the moon is a sphere, like a ball, the sun can only shine on half of it. When we see a full moon in the sky, that means that the sun is behind us, lighting the side of the moon. we can see. A half moon tells us that the sun is off to the side and only shining on half of the moon facing us. Sometimes people call the back side of the moon the dark side. The back side

This is a view of a moon crater from close up.

is that part of the moon we never see because the moon always faces us one way, and the dark side is that part in shadow.

The surface of the moon looks a lot like a desert, except there are no plants there. Have you ever been to a beach, where instead of pure sand, there was a sort of clay mixed with the sand? If you were to take that kind of dust or sand or beach or whatever you call it and spread it over the desert, it would resemble the surface of the moon. Then, of course, there are many craters on the moon. And there isn't any water and there isn't any air.

Don't get me wrong. We were not taking pictures and making observations all the time. We did get enough sleep. We would roll out our sleeping bags and tie the strings at each end to something so that we wouldn't float around. Then we would just climb in and go to sleep.

Then came what I sometimes think was the best part of the trip. Jim and Dave left the ship in the lunar module and landed on the moon. So I got rid of them for a few days and it was really fun. Not that we were enemies by this time, but the inside of the spacecraft is very small. And the three of us were really jammed in. As a matter of fact, when we strapped in with our shoulder belts and waist belts on the morning of launch, we had to overlap shoulders. The area is so small that there wasn't enough room for all of us to get in and relax. It's that tight.

So after four days of crowding, it was kind of nice to have the command module to myself for a few days. I enjoyed it.

I guess by this time I really didn't want to walk on the moon. I had so much to do on my own that I really felt quite happy being where I was and doing what I did. As a matter of fact, from the scientific standpoint, we probably got more from the lunar orbit part of the flight than we got from the surface part of the flight.

When they landed on the moon, they could look at only a very small area. By being in lunar orbit, I could look all over it. Well, almost all over it. Each time I went around the moon I was on the dark side nearly half the time. I couldn't see any of the surface during that half orbit. And there were times on the back side, when I wasn't in contact with Mission Control because the moon was in the way, when I wondered if there was anybody else there.

Anyway, I saw about 25 per cent of the moon, while they looked at only a very small part. And if I missed something on one revolution, I'd pick it up on the next revolution. It might have been fun to walk on the moon, but as far as the importance of the job went, I was happier with my part of the operation.

While Jim and Dave were on the moon, I made thirty-five orbits. Each one took two hours, and that worked out to about three days. All three of us were in lunar orbit together for an-

Sometimes it's good to be by yourself.

other three days, so I was in orbit for a total of about six days, or seventy-five revolutions. I was pretty busy and only had a chance to look at my partners a couple of times in the three days they were on the surface. I looked at a lot of craters and a lot of the features on the moon that the geologists were interested in. I did some experiments from lunar orbit that they couldn't do on the ground.

I did some mapping of the moon for the map makers. And I took a lot of pictures.

We used cameras that were the same as the ones you buy in the store. The only thing that was special about them was a device to make sure that the film was up against the plate so the pictures would not come out wavy. Of course, we had to put special grease in the gears that wouldn't fly out in the vacuum of space.

I had a TV camera in the command module, but I didn't use it while Dave and Jim were on the surface. I did have a monster of a camera, though. It weighed four hundred pounds and was about six feet long and three feet wide. This camera was able to take pictures of the moon at a height of sixty miles that were so clear that they showed rocks that were no bigger than three feet across. I also had some small cameras with me that were like the cameras tourists use.

When Jim and Dave got back to the spacecraft, they said that walking on the moon was sort of like walking on a beach that was packed solid, but loose enough to dig holes in. They said that it got a little bit dusty and the soil would get on their suits and really rub in so that they couldn't get it out. It was almost like a clay powder.

Because of the slight force of gravity, it was something like walking on a trampoline. You put your feet down and sort of bounced back. They had to make a big adjustment on the moon. It's not the same as walking on the earth, but it is not like being in free space either. By the way, they could jump three or four times farther on the moon than they could on the earth—even with their suits on.

While they were down there, you remember that they put up an American flag on the moon's surface. This was not the

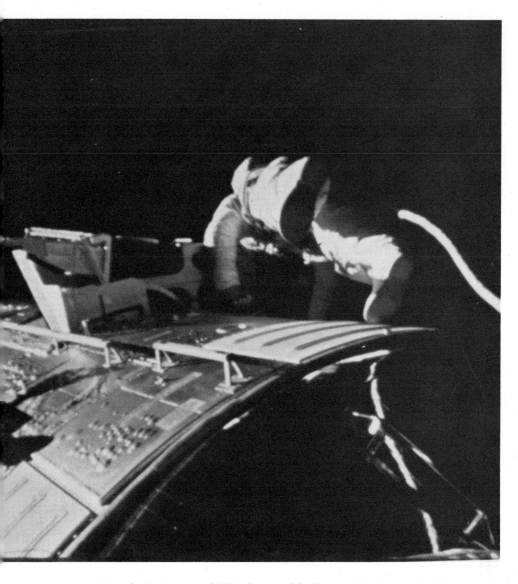

A picture of me during my EVA (extravehicular activity) on the way home. It was taken by Jim Irwin and is the only photograph recovered from the walk.

Jim Irwin saluting the flag in front of the lunar module and the Rover. This is probably the most famous photo of our flight and was taken by Dave Scott.

same as claiming the moon for the United States. There is an international agreement that says that no country can claim the moon. But we wanted people to know we were Americans.

They set up some tiny explosive charges on the moon and measured the explosions with a seismograph. This was not done to blow up the moon. It was to record the shock waves and try to figure out what type of rock is under the surface. The explosive charges were not much more powerful than shotgun shells.

Many things were left on the surface of the moon. There is an experiment station that is still working. There is the descent stage of the lunar module. And the lunar Rover.

We have been accused of being lunar litterbugs. But the plain fact is that there was no way to bring the stuff back with us. We had no room aboard for anything extra except the moon rocks, and we didn't have enough fuel to bring back extra weight.

Many young people seem to be worried most about the Rovers. If another moon flight should ever be attempted, the crew would still probably not recover the Rovers. If you were trying to explore the earth and find out as much as you could about it, how would you do it? You wouldn't go back to the same place every time. You would want to make a trip to America, another to Europe, another to Australia, and so on. If there is another moon flight, the men would not land near a previously explored location.

On the way back I did something that I had really been looking forward to. I got outside the spacecraft. But it turned out not to be as exciting as I thought it would be. I had trained so much for it that when I did it in flight, it was just as if I were still training for it. My heart rate didn't even go up. All I had to think about was just moving around. And I didn't even have to move fast. It was a lot easier than I thought it would be.

While we were in training, I really hadn't thought much about how I would feel when we splashed down. If anything, I thought that I might feel sad that the adventure was over. On the other hand, I might be happy to be back home.

Our splashdown did not turn out to be as routine as we expected. During our final descent one of the parachutes collapsed and we came down a little faster than normal.

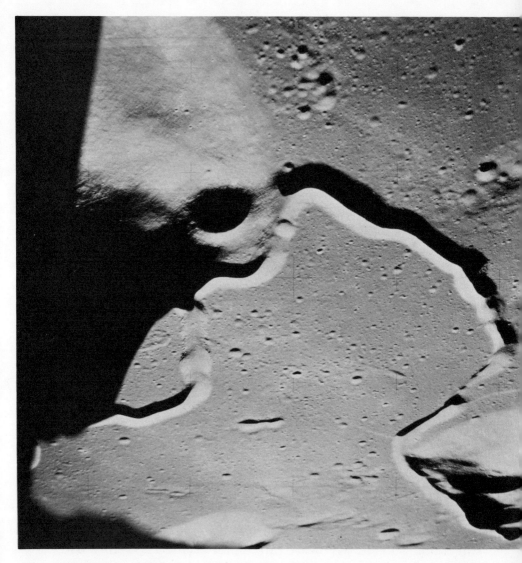

Here is one of my photographs of the Apollo 15 landing site. I was about sixty nautical miles above the surface. The site is about half way between the two crater clusters in the foreground.

We were a little concerned about coming down so fast, but we were lucky. There was no wind blowing us across the surface of the water. So we came right straight down. If there had been any wind that had pushed us along, we would have hit pretty hard. As it was, we didn't splash down much harder than previous flights had.

We went about eight feet into the water when we touched down. And then we came back to the surface and just bobbed about like a cork until the recovery team came and got us.

It is hard to say what I felt like when we hit the water. It was kind of like doing a bellywhopper off a diving board. Except that we were lying on our backs at the time. It happened very fast and then we were sort of floating. It was over so quickly that it is hard to remember what I felt at the time.

And everybody was right there waiting for us. They picked us up in a helicopter and rushed us back to the carrier.

One nice thing about our flight was that we did not have to go into isolation. Other Apollo crews had had to stay locked up alone on the carrier until the doctors were sure that they had not picked up any germs on the moon. By the time of Apollo 15, it was found that there aren't any viruses on the moon that can be brought back. So all we did on the carrier was rest, have physical examinations, and eat steak. We hadn't had any steak for two weeks.

There was a bit of readjustment that we had to go through, though. The first thirty minutes back on earth were pretty shaky. It's more than just getting your land legs back after a sea voyage. It's almost as if for some reason your body is disconnected between your head and your legs. You have to think about putting one foot in front of the other because you haven't done it in twelve days. You haven't had to think about walking. It seems that the automatic mechanism that makes you walk goes to sleep, and you have to wake it up.

Of course, we had no problems communicating with other people when we returned. But it took about a week for our bodies to adjust to the one G here on earth.

For instance, our hearts hadn't worked against gravity for twelve days. So they got very lazy. It took three or four days for

The photo of the final descent of the command module showing the collapsed parachute.

Recovery operations.

Welcome aboard.

Here I am on the U.S.S. *Okinawa.*

the muscle in my heart to get in tune so that it didn't beat faster than normal. My heart rate normally runs about sixty-five beats per minute. When they first recorded it after the flight, it was beating about one hundred twenty per minute. It was so used to not having to do much work to pump the blood around, that it had to make an extra effort now.

We tried to move around as much as possible when we got back. The more exercise you get, the quicker your muscles, especially the heart, get back to normal. We did isometrics and isotonic exercises. Of course, we had done these on the flight. But the problem is that without gravity working against the heart, we had to exercise much harder and longer in space than we would on earth for the same effect.

There are many things that the doctors have not figured out about the effects of space travel on the human body, or even on the human mind. They have no frame of reference. It's a whole new world of science.

What's going to happen next in space? I'm not sure that anybody knows. When my flight was completed in August 1971, there were only six more flights scheduled. Apollos 16 and 17 would finish up the lunar exploration program. Then a new space program called Skylab would start. This program was to test the effects of long duration space flight on man. The crews would live in a large laboratory, placed in earth orbit, for periods up to seventy-five days. After Skylab, the remaining scheduled flight was to be a joint project with the Russians, called ASTP (Apollo-Soyuz Test Project). The purpose of the ASTP is to demonstrate a space-rescue capability between American and Russian spacecraft. To do this we will dock an Apollo command and service module with a Soyuz spacecraft while both are in earth orbit. After docking, the crews will visit each other for a short time, then return to their own spacecraft and re-enter the earth's atmosphere.

You could probably put the Russian cosmonauts and the American astronauts in the same room and not be able to tell them apart. Unless you listened to the language they were speaking. We are all the same kind of people.

But the Russians fly a little differently from us. They build their spacecraft in a different way, too. Their spacecraft are built so that everything can be controlled from the ground. Our spacecraft are built so that everything has to be done in flight by the astronauts. Only the launch is directed from the ground. This means that there is a big difference in the way Russians and Americans approach things.

If we fly with the Russians, they are going to have to do some of their training over here in order to learn to fly our spacecraft. And we will have to do some training over there to learn to fly their spacecraft.

When it comes to the actual flight, I think that they will be the ones to just sit steady. We will be the ones to have to dock with them. The only point of contact between the spacecraft will be the adapters that join the spacecraft together.

Let me say a few words about docking. Our way of going to the moon's surface was to fly two spacecraft, the command module and the lunar module, to lunar orbit. Then we detached the lunar module with two men in it to descend to the surface. When they were finished on the surface, they flew the upper part of the lunar module back into lunar orbit with the command module. The two spacecraft then joined together by what we call "docking." There is a device on the nose of the command module that connects with a matching device on the lunar module. Once the modules are connected, the two men and their equipment and rocks can transfer into the command module, the lunar module can be jettisoned, and the whole crew can come home. The joint American-Russian docking mission will do the same thing, except one of the spacecraft will be Russian.

Who knows, Mars may be next. We've already talked about going there. But Mars is so different an objective from the moon. First of all, we will take a year and a half for the whole flight. That's six months to get there, six months there, and six months back.

We have to start thinking about a whole new thing—a whole new way of living in space. We can go for twelve days—that's fairly easy. We can put all of the supplies we need right on

Mission Control Center, Houston, Texas.

board. But when it comes to sending people up for a year and a half, we have to start thinking about a lot of other things. Where are you going to put all of the stuff they they will need? How much food do you carry for a year and a half? We can't make the food come out exactly according to our requirements even on a twelve-day flight.

And will people ever live on the moon? If they do, it will be years and years from now. Domes would have to be built to contain the air that they would have to breathe. And the air itself would have to be brought from earth. As a matter of fact, we would have to take everything with us. There doesn't seem to be anything on the moon that we can use. And when you start thinking about all of the things that you will have to take with you, you might think that it wouldn't be worth it to have anybody living there permanently.

One last thing. If I had the chance, I would go back. There is a lot of work that has to be done up there. And a lot of things that we have to find out about the moon. Sure, I'd like to go back, especially now that I have had all that training. But let me tell you this. It's nice to be here. The time that I felt the most strange was on the morning after I had spent my first night in my own home. I walked out of the house to get the newspaper and the first thing that I saw was the moon in the sky. What a shock! It's a nice place to visit, but I wouldn't want to live there.

AL WORDEN was born in Jackson, Michigan. After graduating from the United States Military Academy, he was commissioned in the Air Force. He received flight training at Moore Air Base, Texas, Laredo Air Force Base, Texas, and Tyndall Air Force Base, Florida. Prior to his arrival for duty at the Manned Spacecraft Center in Houston, he served as an instructor at the Aerospace Research Pilots School, from which he graduated in 1965. He is also a graduate of the Empire Test Pilots School in Farnborough, England. He attended Randolph Air Force Base Instrument Pilots Instructor School, Texas, and served as a pilot and armament officer with the 95th Fighter Interceptor Squadron at Andrews Air Force Base, Maryland. He has logged more than 3,667 hours flying time—which includes 2,900 hours in jets.

From July 26 to August 7, 1971, Col. Worden served as command module pilot for Apollo 15, the fourth manned lunar landing mission. Col. Worden logged 38 minutes in extravehicular activity outside the command module. He logged 295 hours and 11 minutes in space.

He now lives in California and enjoys bowling, skiing, water skiing, swimming, handball, and automobile racing. He works out of Moffett Air Force Base, near San Francisco.

Rocks, moon, 29, 51
Rogers, Fred, 5, 7
Rotation, earth's, 41
Rover (lunar roving vehicle), 25–29, 41
  described, 25–29
  left behind on moon, 51
  on the moon, 28, 50, 51
  piano-wire tires on, 25
  size and weight of, 25
  slow speed of, 25
Russia, and joint space project with United States, 56–57

Sahara Desert, as seen from space, 41–42
Saturn V space vehicle, lightning striking near, 22
Schmitt, Harrison H., 33
Scott, David R. (Dave), 16, 20, 21, 25, 29, 33, 40, 41
  and landing on the moon, 25, 29, 40, 41, 46–51
  as mission commander, 33
Seat belts, use in space of, 40
Seismograph, use of, 51
Sensors, medical, 29–30
Service module, 18, 56
Shrimp salad, as space food, 32
Sky, color of, as seen from space, 40–41
Skylab space program, 56
Slayton, Donald K., 33
Sleep, in space, 45–46
Sleeping bags, 46
Solar orbit, 20–21
Solid wastes, disposal in space of, 33
South America, as seen from space, 42
Soviet Union. See Russia
Soyuz spacecraft, Russian, 56–57
Space, future programs and living in, 57–58
Space food sticks, 32
Space rescue capability, 21, 56–57
  Joint American-Russian project and, 56–57
Space suits, 29, 30–31, 34
  checking pressure of, 35
  color of, 30–31
  kinds of, 29
  putting on, 30
  weight of, 29
Space travel, future of, 56–59
Splashdown, 51–53, 54
Stages, rocket. See Rockets
Stars, 40

Sunlight (sun's rays), 40
  brightness of the moon and, 44
  color of space suits and, 30–31
Suprathermal ion detector experiment, 27
Survival training, emergency, 24, 25

Time, keeping check of, in space, 40
Tower(s)
  escape, 25
  launch, 21–25

Underwear, kind used in space, 29–30
United States
  and international agreement on moon claims, 51
  and joint space program with Russia, 56–57
United States Air Force, 12
United States Military Academy (West Point), 11–12, 13

Viruses (germs), and moon flight, 53

Wastes. See Body wastes; solid wastes
Water, drinking, and space flight, 31–32
Weight, 39–40
Weightlessness, 40, 42
West Point. See United States Military Academy (West Point)
Women, as astronauts, 17
Worden, Alfred M., 61
  background, birth, childhood, education, 10, 11–14, 16
  biographical note, 61
  joins Air Force, 12–14
  and moon flight, 16–33
    See also Moon flight
  selection and training for Apollo 15 mission, 16–33
  start of interest in becoming an astronaut, 12–14
  at West Point, 11–12, 13
Worden, Mrs. Alfred M. (wife), 14
Worden, Alison (daughter), 14, 15
Worden, Carolyn (sister), 10, 11, 12
Worden, Helen C. (mother), 11, 12
Worden, Jerry (brother), 11, 12
Worden, Merrill (daughter), 14, 15
Worden, Merrill B. (father), 11, 12
Worden, Peter (brother), 11, 12
Worden, Sally (sister), 10, 11, 12

Zero-G environment, 42

64